when flowers wilt

manya mehta

ILLUSTRATED BY RHEA MEHTA

First Published in November 2021

ISBN: 978-93-5472-159-5

BLUEROSE PUBLISHERS

www.bluerosepublishers.com

info@bluerosepublishers.com

+91 8882 898 898

Cover Design:

Shreya Kapoor

Typographic Design:

Tanya Raj Upadhyay

Distributed by: BlueRose, Amazon, Flipkart

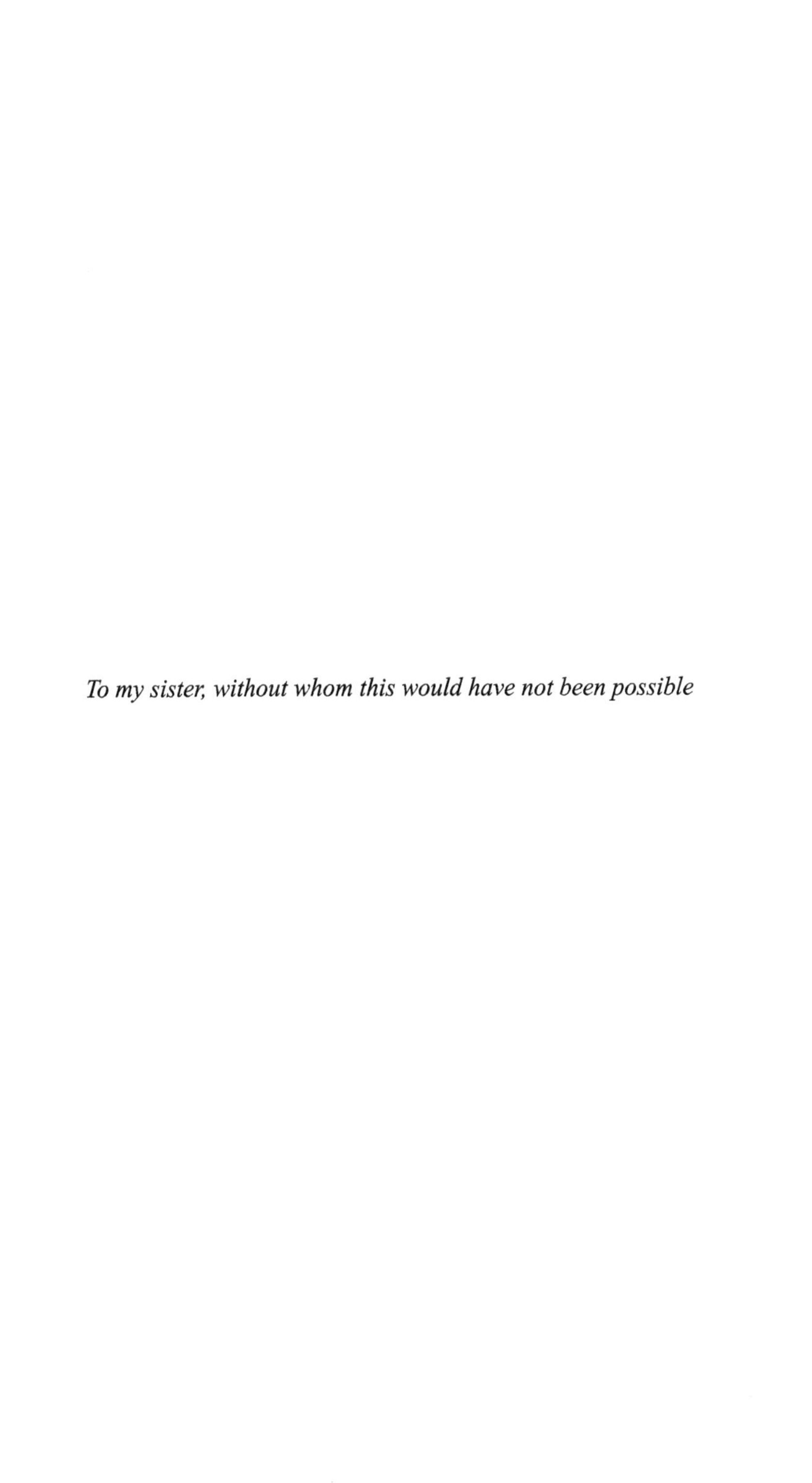

To my sister, without whom this would have not been possible

Acknowledgements

I would like to express my gratitude towards my parents for always believing in me, even during the moments I did not believe in myself. Without their constant support and encouragement, I would not be who I am today. I would like to thank my sister for not only making the impeccable artwork for this book, but for staying up till four am on weekends re-reading every draft of every poem I wrote. And more importantly, for helping me make this idea come to life. I would like to thank my friends for always being the best support system. Thank you for always being my rock, you know who you are. A special thank you to Aadvik – my biggest supporter.

Contents

1. Doldrums....1
2. hell is a beautiful place with you 2
3. silas's first love....3
4. The flame which demolished me 4
5. my lesions in song 5
6. apple picking at the bergamo orchard....6
7. the coffee roasters of palo alto 7
8. marlboro....8
9. seven memories of you 9
10. what once was 10
11. One day you will find me....11
12. how to write a poem....12
13. 11 years 13
14. growing is normal, growth is rare....14
15. two people die every second....15
16. wilhem....16
17. what hephaestion left his lover 17
18. when we said goodbye....18
19. when i saw you....19
20. the casualties of our love....20
21. what we choose to remember....21
22. melancholy and you....22
23. but since when did life need a reason?....23
24. death is in love with life....24
25. your heart doesn't know pain....26
26. her 27
27. why i miss you 28
28. her anatomy....29
29. oxytocin....30

30. capricorn moon 31
31. she broke me and i'm grateful 32
32. heartbreak doesn't care about your gender 34
33. sometimes my heart sings in grief 35
34. why shakespeare loved tragedies 36
35. fairytales aren't fiction 37
36. Lay flowers beside her grave 38
37. the thorn filled garden behind the white picket fence 39
38. the butterflies are jealous 40
39. the moon is a hopeless romantic 42
40. Why Saturn hates Mars 44
41. She resembles a ray of sunlight, ...44
42. black fills my skies 45
43. a domino effect in the sky 46
44. the burden of the rain 47
45. the seasons are confused 48
46. black fills my skies vol. 2 / "my haunting black shadow" 49
47. the ghosts of summer 50
48. the sun is falling asleep 51
49. i broke my own heart by mistake 52
50. alcohol within your lips 53
51. misery loves company (and i love you) 54
52. terminal lucidity 55
53. death became her 56
54. why women kill 57
55. practically lethal in every way 58
56. cry me a river & i'll dry it out 59
57. gaslight 60
58. da vinci was a fraud 61
59. when you reach the end of this poem, let her memory go 62

60. Five questions I don't want you to answer 63
61. a night at windy pharaoh..64
62. sharks 65
63. From Slovakia 66
64. the tea vendors of new delhi 68
65. red riding hood with a gun 69
66. game...70
67. the times in which my perfect gpa cannot help............................71
68. king 72
69. scars...73
70. Flaming butterflies 74
71. lust, passion, love...75
72. when your flowers have wilted and the sun has said its goodbyes .76
73. Pâtisserie Amandine...78
74. A Sunday morning in an all American diner...............................80
75. Eclipse 81

Doldrums

mud engulfs the white noise which surrounds
your duplicity drenches the motors of the old town cars
the buildings resort to a state of vexation, standing tall and proud
a tornado of fury casts a shadow on the fire of the stars

black tar soaks into the lungs of this city's pride
the grass turns a shade of ochre, the soil now a deep blue
the barks of the trees crumble and leaves frisk to hide
my spine attacked by reminiscence of times with you

the rain now replaced by sulphuric acid
the winds carry gravel and cement
the redolent scents now reek acrid
the crowd stripped of their adolescence

for the dust has now settled
petals dotted with blood and stains
store windows cracked and pelted
and misery is all that remains

— melancholy strikes this town.

hell is a beautiful place with you

the dust settles on these molten rocks
the pores in my skin blaze with envy
these doors bound us, seal with a metal lock
the flames grow stronger, the air more deadly

we ignite this land of fire with our own flame
the scorching skies show mercy to our home
singed rivers and scalding clouds leave a stain
my skin crinkles, your fingertips turn to stone

fueled by evil inclination, discoloured land remains
my blood boils, but with you, hell is a beautiful place
the thorn filled gardens resemble those of eden
the constraints set on us reek nothing but freedom
there are tall towers of black, of evil, of torture, of revenge, of cold
but when i see them through your eyes, they appear made of gold

hell is a beautiful place with you, and only you
we were sent here to suffer, burn like the stars
yet we took the evil and together *we made it ours*

silas's first love

she crucifies his intent, purges his purity
idolises this situation of senseless absurdity
when they were fifteen, they first locked eyes
and in an instance, silas fell for her foolishly
the red smeared on her lips masked the white lies
and so, this descendant of lucifer found her disguise

the fire burnt his skin, the sun lit her candles
they found home in the meadow by the lake
fox-trotting on the creaky wooden panels

pellets of sweat dripped down his face when she was near
for silas didn't fall often, but when he did, he fell for years

she abandoned silas at the home they created
his first love left him hopelessly captivated
for she left him with all the pain he could withstand
and now, she must escape, blood is at her hands

The flame which demolished me

His touch was like a black sea
of fear, greed and hatred
spreading through your naked skin
corrupting what is sacred

His touch lingered lesser
than he would have liked
But his touch prevailed forever
and remained after you wiped

His fingers like thorny ropes
capturing your innocent soul
hurting your pure skin
cutting your pure mind

His gaze like a burning knife
cutting through all your defences
and burning the inside will
setting alight your desire to live

my lesions in song

regret lingers, lacing my discombobulated thoughts
you chastised my senses, engulfed me in your taunts
denounced my moments of glee, turned me bitter
provoked my insecurity and teased, pushing my trigger
for now i am resentful of the melodies you made me hear
the dulcet harmonies which estranged me from fear
and since you played me with your chords all along
now you sit here and listen to my lesions in song

apple picking at the bergamo orchard

the scent of citrus-filled lemons slowly drowns out
the sight of fruits on each tree grows in number
as you progress further down this isolated route
you will soon find yourself standing under
— *a municipality of apple trees*

the bergamo orchard never lost its charming manner
every tree trunk holds the spine of new lives
the atmosphere grows more timid, silencing the clamour
for now, you are amongst the raging ants and beehives

within the crowded green leaves, we spot small dots of red
each long-pointed branch holds its own prized possession
these fruits were a result of envy, nature's natural progression
the sun punished the trees and into these small dots they bled
and so, we see a mountain of apple trees as we look ahead

the land outside this place is stained with humanity,
as our skies have been left grey and rivers left tortured
yet every now and then we find a moment of sanity
when we go apple picking at the bergamo orchard

the coffee roasters of palo alto

when i was seventeen i was in love with the ocean
when i turned eighteen i fell in love with a girl
when i turned nineteen i tried finding myself
now, at twenty, i see reality in the world

the summer of 92, spent with those two strange men
the aroma of their drink traveling down the entire street
luring in every bystander with the undeniable scent
of their columbian brewed light coffee beans

the sun never set there, and the city never slept
the waves drowned me in their power
the caffeine cravings often left me swept

every evening at seven pm the sun would say its goodbyes
we'd gather by a fire and greet the moon with our eyes
for every day was the same, yet so very different
every week spiked boredom, yet overwhelming interest

if only we could go back to the days we spent by sea
as we sipped cold brew and smoked bright leaf tobacco
sitting in the rain with the coffee roasters of palo alto

marlboro

wind coats the riverbed of this grey norwegian coast
the summer skies are being haunted by winter's ghost

the political situation grows more volatile
the state of the country descending into turmoil

but we find happiness in these crisp summer evenings
i dress head to toe in red, his smile now beaming

he entices me with chaos, provokes me with tumult
i make him full of envy, his gestures grow more violent

he waits for me every morning
as he stands by the door of the chateau
lighter in hand, lips tasting of marlboro

seven memories of you

a cassette tape of billy joel, the one you gifted me for my seventeenth
every melody we listened to with the stars above, the seaside sand
underneath

an empty photo frame, for we said we'd fill it when we made our home
yet that day never came, our raging passion now turning into stone

an unused pack of chewing gum, the one i bought before your long flight
yet it is left untouched, like our thoughts after every heated fight

a broken wine glass, the one that shattered when it hit the rigid table
like the time you broke my trust, for after that our story turned fatal

a novel of your poetry, every word strung together by your whimsical
rhymes
the one you shared with me at the meadow, stories of your favourite crimes

a brooch from my grandmother, the one i showed you on new year's day
when we kissed in hopes for the future and made promises to always stay

an over-used blue tea kettle, piping hot water seeping out of the sides
the day you left me with these seven memories and a miserable goodbye

what once was

a bottle of champagne coated with your regret
a half-lit cigarette coated in all my miserable mistakes
ombre wooden frames engulfed in our distress
the wet mud soaked in sympathy by our spot at the lake

your image, tainted in my paintings by their portrayal
this desire, inexplainable, alluding to the dread
sacrificial stars, causalities of our betrayal
the wet mud, soaked in pity, surrounds the riverbed

shattered pieces of our story, put back together with trust
this awful circumstance, of remembering what once was

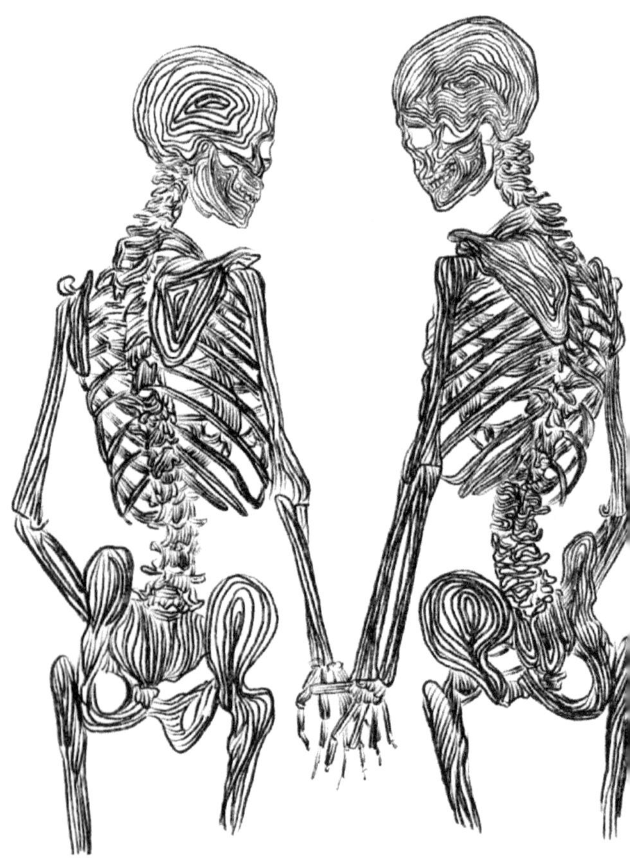

One day you will find me

Wait for me before the sun sets,
the golden atmosphere keeping us company
the noisy streets echoing ambient laughter
the dust settling down after an afternoon of wind
for we can breathe in each other's presence,
and admire the shifting colours in the sky.

Wait for me before dawn strikes,
the moon sheltering our discomfort with light
the silence provoking our inner thoughts to reveal
the emptiness of isolation dejecting our joy
for we can be just us with no one around,
and not a thing to interrupt the mellow surroundings.

Wait for me during the early afternoons,
the ones where birds are chirping loud and proud,
the ones where children are crowded in playgrounds,
the ones where your mother goes apple-picking,
the ones where everyone is preoccupied with daily tasks
for we can get ready for the day to come together,
and be hopeful of the future which we share.

Wait for me where we first met under the oak tree,
the one with our initials carved into its spine
the one with leaves trickling down every other minute
the one with deep sunken roots holding our past
the one with our beginning and the one with its end
for we can remember the good old days,
and admire the stars while we fall in love all over again.

Wait for me, wherever or whenever you do it,
for neither of us are ready to let go.
And I'll search for you along the way, from land to sea
hopeful for the day, the one day you will find me.

how to write a poem

to begin, come up with your most creative rhymes
perhaps rhyme together with feather or nine with time

next, remember your most aching emotions
heartbreak, passion, insecurity, commotion

and so, put the words onto paper with your pen of choice
and maybe add a few adjectives, adjust the tone of your voice

when you talk about *her,* do it with vagueness, mention *him* without a name
for they can be anything you want, a metaphor for the sea or the rain

and if you want to be unique, add an inconsistent rhyming scheme
format it as a haiku, skip words and phrases, make colours into themes

write about the time you saw a lion or about the fastest cars
for at the end of it, no matter what you're left with — *it will still be a poem.*
the poem will not be perfect, but the poem will still be *yours.*

11 years

we have 11 years to escape the burden of regret
11 years to preserve, 11 years to pay our debt
we have 11 years to restore natural order
6 years to save your mother, 5 to save your daughter

11 years before we let down she who gave us life,
11 years until the blood will be dripping from your knife

they say after 11 years the impact of climate change will be irreversible
for our machinery and technology may be, but our land is not submersible

now as concern is avoided, temperatures have started to rise
when in a state of war, every country in the UN frisks to become allies
yet when such an issue is brought up, not a mumble is to be heard
but the blame will be on you and i, at the end of these next 11 years

growing is normal, growth is rare

we all grow.

our waists get wider, hands get bigger, and legs get longer
our brains get wiser, skin gets rougher, and muscles get stronger

since the age of six, i was always told that if someone crossed me while i was
laying down i would not grow any taller
and so, every time my cousins crossed me i'd chase them all over the house
in the fear i'd always feel smaller

my mother used to mark my height
on our blank white wall with a pencil
inch by inch my height varied more,
and my emotions became more inessential

by the age of ten, i was no longer a happy little girl anymore, i had grown
my loud elated laughs had now turned into low irritated groans

the flower by my window grew a new petal yesterday
a beautifully curved surface of pink with little details of grey
the grass often grows too long for the liking of our feet
and so gardeners trim and trim, for this garden is now complete

we are surrounded with growth
we see it in our flowers, our trees, our art
yet we succumb to the neglect
when this growth comes within the heart

for growing is normal, *but growth is rare*
we all grow in size, yet a few learn to care

two people die every second

on an average, every second the world holds two people less,
just like that, it's now four, six, eight, ten—chaos makes its mess
every second you take for granted; another's blood turns blue
and the stars cast their shadow, for the skies gain something new

now fourteen, sixteen, eighteen, it goes on
but the sun will still gleam, there will still come dawn
the world works in a strange way, flaunting its crime
for every moment we feel happiness, every still in time
is a moment ending the significance of another's life

we could find beauty in each other's words
our heart could be torn apart by another
our smiles could be wide enough to be heard
we could be fighting our thoughts away from a past lover

yet in this very moment, as the clock ticks forward
to another soul, nothing is important anymore
so it sings in harmony, nature takes its course

every second the world holds two less people
thirty, thirty-two, thirty-four.

wilhem

long dark hair punctured with coruscating particles
dimples on each cheek, winsome and prominent
for his smile cures the dying embers in the grate
his eyes widen, the flicker in his pupils fulgurate
his eyebrows furrow in deception, each hair stands at a still
his nose resembles the pointiest mountains, his lips mirror the hills

his ears replicate the curves of the moon,
his collar bones skewer out of his shoulders,
for his laughter cures the heat during June
his frown brings the winds of December closer

the delicate dotting on his skin epitomises every tragedy
and until he says the words, the storm will still come
the beetles and the moths hide behind the forest canopy
for when he says the words, nature will finally succumb
and until that day, *for wilhem i leave this rhapsody*

what hephaestion left his lover

a song of sorrowful regret
a postcard painted with greed
the anthology of their insidious threats
the remains of the macedonia maple trees

a painting made with his tears
the fossils of their nights spent in rage
sounds of loud laughter and elated cheers
the mourning of loss after the plague

a pen and stash of ink moulded with their pride
the white bedsheets and a torn mattress cover
the aftermath of what's left, once his blood dried
for demise ended their connection,
and all that remains is *what hephaestion left his lover*

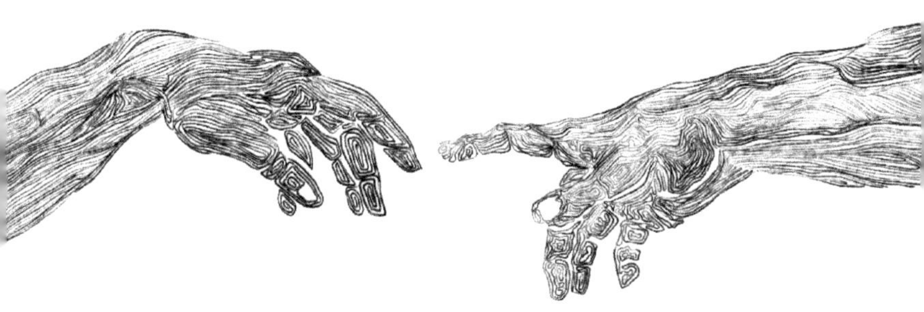

when we said goodbye

when we said goodbye, the sun dimmed its light
the clattering dishes on my shelf started to crack
the grass grew yellow, the clouds abandoned the night
birds stopped chirping; the wind left a stain of black

when we said goodbye, my heartbeat slowed down
my impulses grew stronger, my blood mourned the loss
my purple bruises paralleled the fruits as they browned
my brain lost all control, for my memories of you got lost

when we said goodbye, this town became abandoned
the streetlights no longer greeted me on my daily walks
the concrete roads rusted, and the paths left me stranded
for i was isolated by these buildings for creating this chaos

when we said goodbye, the sky turned grey
the flowers wilted; the river stopped moving
treasure lost value, gold turned to clay
our actions left the whole world disapproving

just to remember the feeling, now i write about you and i draw you,
when we said goodbye, i remembered the first time *when i saw you.*

when i saw you

when i saw you i forgot how to hate
the sunlight became more warm
my body parts lost all weight

when i saw you, the wind danced around me
the petals on the flowers beside us grew taller
the feeling of being hopeful drowned me

when i saw you, angels came down from heaven
my cellphone started to buzz, my earrings began to click
rain rushed down to see us meet, staining the bright orange brick

when i saw you, the fruits on my tree became more sweet
i found beauty in tiny insects, i found love in language
my heartbeat quickened, my body felt more complete

the world around me changed, we modified the skies
and hopefully, i remember this moment when we say goodbye.

the casualties of our love

the english language forgot how to punctuate
the nicotine fell out of every robusto cigar
the strongest hurricanes began to abate
physicists lost the location of every known star
mathematicians forgot the calculations of pi
chloroplasts vanished from every flower cell
meteorologists could not locate the rainfall of july
white noise came from every ringing bell

for some day i will forget you, and you will forget me
but i will always remember you when i see
broken land beneath me or red skies above
everything in the world will remain a casualty of our love

what we choose to remember

our past lovers do not define us
the heartbreak we weaved our days through
the tears we stained our clothes with
the hope we let fall into the shower drain as we washed away our sins

our past mistakes do not haunt us
our entire existence does not depend on that one event
the incident, the accident we choose to underline
we chose to keep it in bold and the rest of our accomplishments in lowercase

our past failures do not hold us back
all the dreams we let fall down our bodies onto the ground
all the times it wasn't us succeeding but it was our darkness, it will not stop us from trying again
after all, the scars on our skin have a lost cause needing to be redeemed

our past friendships do not restrict us
all the lies looking us in the face and challenging us to trust again
the memories you swallow for breakfast and let out in your thoughts at night
find friendship in the mirror, the one who looks back at you everyday

our past aches do not burn us anymore
for we see no harm in a little blood or pity from the rain
every tear we see in our eyes reflects a time when we were stronger
it flows down our faces to remind us of the stone in our bodies called muscles

our past fantasies do not drown us anymore
we know better, the world engulfs all dreamers and spits them out
the fantasy we seek is no longer a reality we hope for
we understand the significance of life and fiction

our past is no longer trapping us
we grow, arm's length, our minds are now stronger

the past is forgotten, for better.
the past is forgotten, for worse.

melancholy and you

i wish i never fell for you, the fall was more of a crash
my fingers covered in blood and skin covered in ash
countless promises later, you left without a care
now i'm left with what i feared, pity and despair
the only two things i have, to remember you by
melancholic emotions, the ones that i despise

i see a pale reflection in the mirror, my blood turns blue
here i sit alone, with melancholy and memories of you

but since when did life need a reason?

sunlight dawns on her skin in his presence
his disingenuous smile leaves her conflicted
the memories they create mirror her adolescence
his intentions spew anger and bleed wicked

her life became him, his not quite the same
her heart succumbed to the pressure
his darkness took this as a new game
his gold was iron, disguised as treasure
her happiest moments were those spent in pain

dewdrops of tears covered her eyes in guilt
ambient voices disassociated her from reality
melancholy burdened her as now her flowers wilt
he left her with abundant ache and no concrete clarity

but since when did blood need a body to flow in
since when did breath need lungs to be held in
since when did bones need fluid to grow in
since when was murder not revenge but a crime
since when did every second passing increase the time
since when did leaves clatter during a change in season

but since when did life need a reason?

death is in love with life

once there lived two long lost lovers, bounded by broken hope
it is impossible for the two to exist together, divided by a rope
yet their hearts squirm for each other, moments replayed of each glance
their souls scream in mutual chaos, for the day when the two meet in chance

for death and life are hopeless lovers, weaker and stronger
the manic in their tangled past memories that still live along

but eventually, life accepts the refusal; she lets go of the what if
after all, she lives on the sound idea of reality, away from the memory of his
while death holds back life and her charismatic free spirit, he stays greedy
his bruised knees stain the grounds as his fingers fidget to be needy

like all forbidden lovers, life tries her best to fight as she gets away
yet she always finds herself coming back to him, acceptance, she's his prey

the moment strikes her spine, realisation peaks within
death is inevitable; there is no getting rid of him
they're stuck in this cycle; everlasting but so it seems,
death wishes to live the life that she gleams,
he wants the overwhelming emotions and joy life receives.

hopelessly in love, yet the two are kept apart by each breath
but this tragedy grows weaker when one with life chooses death

for that split second, they have a gun against their head, in blood, they lay
life meets death: and now the option of suicide grows popular day by day
the youth possessing longer lives, choose to end it, thoughts spiral
love is an evil emotion, it's the unspoken eighth sin in the bible
lust, gluttony, greed, sloth, wrath, envy, pride and now love,
for hell is in love with heaven, demons from below and angels from above
life starts to drive people to death; she makes them choose that path
and so there live two long lost lovers, reunited at last.

the next generation evolves weaker in mental health, feelings scope broader
most of the children now need medication for all types of anxiety disorders
death is now labelled as an escape for feeling pain, people idealise the thought
so the rope comes out of the drawer, battles are no longer meant to be fought

and so these hopeless lovers get to be together, they share moments before the dying fire turns into hard coal
in this matter, a love story some may call it, perspective plays a paramount role

47,185 people choose to kill themselves every year,
but to the two lovers, its 47,185 seconds together, a moment near

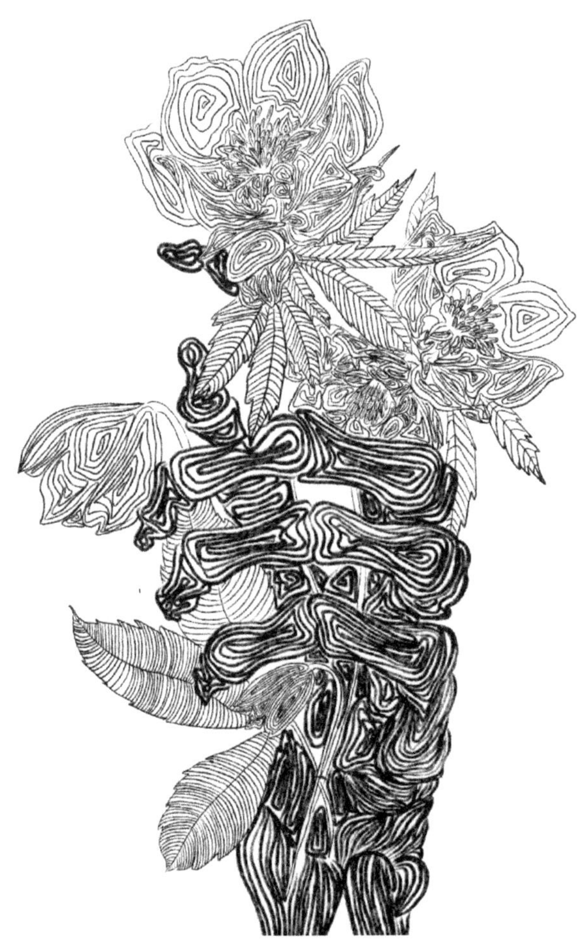

your heart doesn't know pain

your heart is made for the sole purpose of beating your blood
yet people describe sadness as an emotion sparked from their chest
your heart craves his smile like he craves his favourite drug
sorrow fills in the pits of your stomach, your arteries protest

your heart is not sad, it's your mind that holds a toll on you
your heart is not sad, your lungs haven't slowed down

your emotions are not misplaced,
your ears aren't hearing sounds
this darkness is created
within the depths of your mind
a whole world finding causes
for symptoms that you don't feel

but our minds control our bodies,
they can create pain where they want
for we live feeling what we think
with every short breath losing count

the walls of your arteries have no space for grief
just like the other four chambers in your heart
unbothered by your surroundings,
the arrogant comment he made
your mind is the one who notices this
your mind is the one that feeds on your insecure thoughts
your conscience joins in, and the three tear you apart

no, our white blood cells have no fighting mechanism against our own senses
and so, we live thinking, explaining, blaming, hating our *broken* hearts.

her

he loves when i wear my black halter top
with bows on its edges, cuts on each of the sides
a high hemline, a low-cut neck, sleeves that are wide

he hates when i wear my old worn-out sweater
with stitches of blue hearts, sleeves that cover my skin
a turtleneck by the shoulders, a thick woollen rim

he likes to show me off when i'm in my pleated skirt
proudly walks past all the men, my thighs exposed
my waist cinched in, making sure to keep my legs closed

he hides me from his friends when i wear my favourite jeans
they are baggy from the thighs, ripped on the knees, wide from the ankles
the waist too big to fit without a belt, the strings sticking out dangle

for he loves when I'm *her*, but he hates when I'm *me*.

why i miss you

every time someone asks why i miss you
i say fresh oranges and cinnamon
cream cheese, a strawberry cigarette
a half-full bottle of sauvignon blanc wine
petals and rosemary, a banana crust pie
drops of rainfall, the clouds crowding the sky
the scent of the ocean, a minced spicy chicken
or the rainbow beside a puree of lemons

i say heated fudge brownies, the
smell of home, shredded breadcrumbs over
a bourbon pecan pork, a sprinkle of cocoa
on creme brûlée french toast.

i add on, the sunset and herbal tea,
the strength of black coffee
violets and daisies, almond on ice cream
cookies made with oatmeal and
alfredo penne pasta with shredded bacon bits
my favourite avocado wrap or
dozens of white bread toasts along
with jam and peanut butter spread
an isle of pomegranate, a touch of lime

that's how you tasted, every single time.
you taste like love, you taste like passion
you taste like happiness but,
out of all the things my palate felt,
every flavour you brought to my tongue
most of all, you tasted like *freedom.*

— *why i miss you*

her anatomy

the veins on her back join to build a map of a forbidden town
each tangle of her hair lays like a wave against the small of her neck
every scar knots into a storybook telling a tale that's cursed bitter
her eyes look at me as if the sun would dare to shine brighter
her breath replicates anxious clouds heaving before a storm
her smile corrodes the evil, it ribbons into a perfectly curved moon
the dimples near her nose crinkle like crushed flowers, clustered and petite
every speck of every freckle gives you a reason to hope again
her fingers, though crooked and long, resemble the tallest towers
her collarbones straight as spikes of rain falling to their death on the ground
her jawline fitting a love letter for the ones who dare to dream
the curve in her ear giving direction to the ones who find themselves lost
her arms dangle in sync, spell out a melody rich in rhythm,
the beauty spot near her eye frames her face like a diamond does a finger
the birthmark on her thigh resembles a droplet of silk in miles of dust
when she asks me what i love about her, i say everything, she laughs
shakes her head at me like i have no definite answer, little does she know
when someone asks me what i love about her, i reply *her anatomy*

oxytocin

flowers wilt when the sunshine leaves them at the alter
death has become cheap, three cigarettes come for a dollar
noisy streets are silenced when the moon returns to its place
crime finds a safe haven, the dark shelters it in its embrace

adrenaline and dopamine fuel your quivering hands
you hesitantly exhale, smoke fills around the land
you pity yourself and wallow in your dejection
you turn to substance to cure you of this rejection
cocaine, ecstasy, alcohol, you finally cave
but in reality, it is oxytocin that you crave

for you try to replicate the feeling *of me*,
the same butterflies travelling down your spine
yet the high will eventually become a low,
and your darkness will cave into the memory of my smile

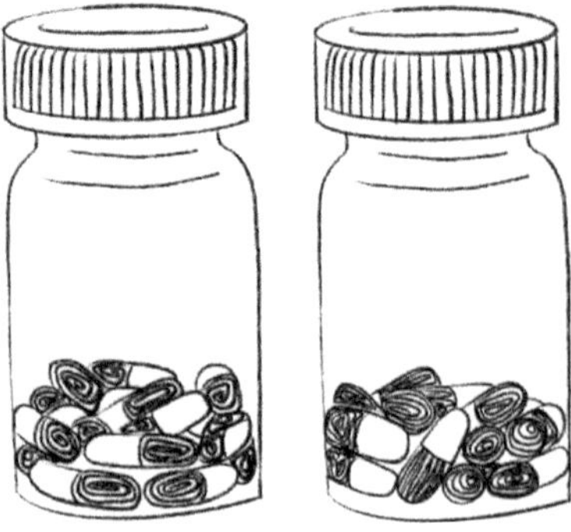

capricorn moon

discomfort seeks shelter from the rain
for the gloomy days have a sense of security
ink drops coat the wet pages with stains
the words of the poem i wrote you soak in impurity

every inch out of place craves my attention
for a comfortable home is one which is consistent
and when my anger builds up frustrated tension
i resort to my natural state, envious and distant

yearning for stability, grounded like the earth
full of rage like fire, denounced by my worth
tiny shining stars create the map of my pattern
for the day i was born, the crescent was ruled by saturn

she broke me and i'm grateful

the bittersweet words still resurface into my thoughts
her embracing laugh still is one i cannot resist
the pits of my stomach ache and my heartbeat rots
as i recall the feeling of when we last kissed

it's been three months since i've been in her presence
smelt her scent, touched her skin, heard her voice
i see her in the moon, her smile through the crescent
every syllable not from her mouth is one of strepitous noise

it's been five months since we sat at the garden by the river
my body feels bruised as my blood circulation is at a still
i cannot go a moment without feeling her beside me, a slight shiver
the flower by the window now flaccid, the sunlight more dim

it's been six months since my heart has been broken
i received a voice mail from her to gather my things
yet i cannot get myself to face her, not a word to be spoken
so, i let the numbness fill me as the cellphone repeatedly rings

it's been a year now since she left me. i've learnt to let go,
my feelings for her are now in the past, the present is all i see
sometimes she finds her way into my thoughts when i see the moon glow
but when dawn approaches, everything is restored for now the sun gleams

it's been two years and i have healed, my stomach doesn't ache at her name
and if i wanted her to suffer i'd raise my finger and point blame
yet heartbreak isn't about the bitter, but rather it is about the sweet,
for now, my blood flows in and out of my veins, a full circulation complete

this is my love letter to you
because the moon will always remind me of your smile.
but once i find my soulmate, i will know because she will me by sun.
my world doesn't revolve around you, yet you remain in my skies
it's been three years now and all my hurting has finally been done.

yours truly,
the boy you left broken

(i'm sorry i missed your voice mail)

heartbreak doesn't care about your gender

heartbreak doesn't care about your gender
men are ruthless, women delicate and tender
heartbreak doesn't care about your age, your size, your name
yet as your heart is falling apart, your fingers rise to point blame

boys don't cry and women don't betray
heartbeat left leaden, feelings left grey

your tolerance for pain is not determined by your pronouns
when she cheats, it is because he did something to deserve it
he abused her or he used her, he ignored her or broke his vows

there is no room for men to have feelings in society
the heavy lifters of the home, the ideal shoulder to cry on
mental illness is a myth to men, no sorrow or anxiety
so, he must wipe away his tears and be the body to rely on

in today's world, every broken bond leaves the man to blame for disloyalty
it's her story to tell, and our story to believe, in the process emotions render
for when will they understand, heartbreak doesn't care about your gender

sometimes my heart sings in grief

the last time you visited,

my sufferings moulded into a song

the last time you said you missed me,

the chords strung along

the last time i kissed you goodbye

my heartbeat synchronised

the last time i thought of you,

the notes started to perfectly align

for my heart sings in grief from time to time

it loves to highlight the bitterness of my feelings

and slowly my body gets lost in the rhyme

and the lyrics of this music begin my

h e a *l* i n g

why shakespeare loved tragedies

being in love makes you wonder why the world is so against it
comfort creates curiosity, love often makes one naive
however, i still recall the moment in time that i sensed it
the time my warm feeling of joy turned into a cold pit of grief

you ask, why did shakespeare love tragedies?
the best moments are those spent in affection
yet your promises left me bitter and full of sorrow
i was the remains of your betrayal and neglection

for now, i understand his critiques of a happily ever after
love is simply the mistaken feeling of oxytocin in your veins
there was a time i believed that love was your laughter
but i no longer do, as the sound of silence is what remains

fairytales aren't fiction

you and me, before we became us
condemned to betrayal from the first glance

the same repeating story of two people
for when eve bit the apple,
adam knew it was lethal
and when lady macbeth took her life
her husband did not bat an eye
when josephine was murdered,
it was her lover's blood on the knife
the lord of england himself, could not keep a wife
and so they go, divorced, beheaded, died
divorced, beheaded, survived

for before we could become an us
this story had already turned into one of fatality
as at the end of the day, tyranny beats morality

Lay flowers beside her grave

You cannot touch her skin again,
you cannot be in the presence of her smile.
You cannot feel her grin again,
you cannot wrap yourself around her spine.

You can neglect the love you two shared,
but you cannot abandon the memory of her laugh.
You can dial her number to hear her voice again,
but you cannot pause your heart from splitting in half.

You can visit her at the cemetery
but you cannot hold her in your embrace.
In that moment you accept that you've lost control,
There is not much you can do —
except, *lay flowers beside her grave.*

the thorn filled garden behind the white picket fence

you saved me the day you found me crying by the sainte-croix lake
you sheltered and nurtured and healed me when i wanted to break
and when the times were good, they were paradisiacal in all its sense
but when the times were bad, my feelings were demolished at your expense
for now, the skies are filling with fire and butterflies are filling with rage
the sun is turning into stone and the flowers are turning into black sage
the scars on my back are begging for mercy as they morph into blades
and often when i remember, i wonder why i ever stayed
for now, i know all along, while i came to your defense
you were the thorn filled garden behind the white picket fence

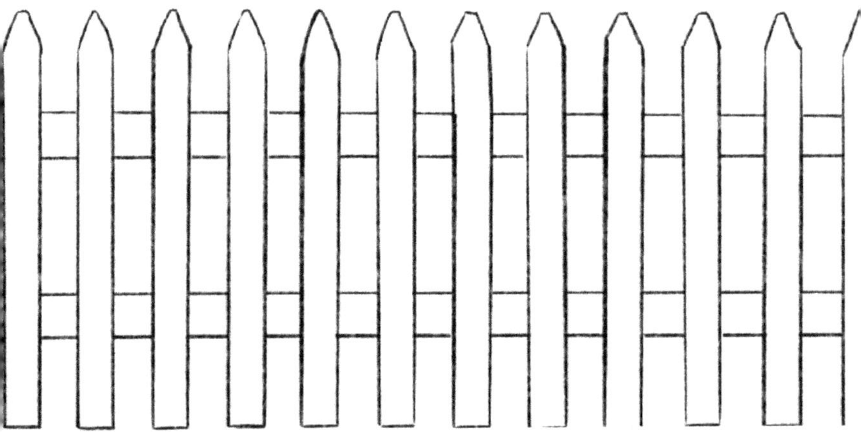

the butterflies are jealous

her wings fled open, revealing the silhouette of the perfect curve
the strings of black spikes create her pattern; straight lines sharp stripes
the blue imitates a dull antique gown yet the brightness seeps through her
every loop of the circles within, reflect the fruit she sits on; ever so ripe
her body flexible as a feather, her head an ant compared to her wings
they spread out in favour of her beauty, the tips of her feet poke to sting

the specks of purple hide, crowding the surface of her very own design
two flimsy rays of the sun, coloured black, form her antennas, spike out of her head
her wings restricted close, touch in an instance as the two perfectly align
her tail, though barely visible, overshadow the striking shape of her, pointed instead
so, they say, butterflies can no longer fly if their wings have been touched
so, they mean, kids can no longer be innocent once harmed, and hushed.

she's an angelic existence, the true form of beauty in nature
she bonds with the flowers, the fruits, the grass, yet not satisfied
the butterflies are jealous she cries, ever since a lonely slug
sex: you may call it, love, the birds and the bees or a special hug.
the butterflies are jealous of the birds and the bees; *for they create life.*
for her sole purpose in this world is to look appealing as she strives
supermodels are never satisfied by just being good looking, or being on the cover page
butterflies do not accept their only purpose to be beauty, for now, her wings fill with rage

her eyes turn a striking red as the flakes of her pupils grow strong
her stinging legs claw down and her wings scream out a raging storm
the antennas on her head are no longer graceful, but now resemble knives
the flowers tremble, they weep "the butterflies are out to get our lives"
a butterfly holds no power once touched, yet we only like to touch what's pretty
young girls must close their legs and wear long skirts to escape the burden of pity

and now she strikes through this storm she has created, her body feeling heavy
it's the birds and the bees who watch her, for they are the ones filling with envy

the moon is a hopeless romantic

the moon told me you were upset
its light shined dark glare
it demonstrated by its crest
the curve rounded by despair
the moon told me you needed me
it circled around my head
its stars intertwined to make me see
every moment i make you dread
the moon called me here
it sunk into my path everyday
it convinced me blind

for the skies are filling with rage
as the moon neglects its place
it keeps running away into your arms
to protect your heart from feeling me
the moon cures the destruction

the galaxy reeked with anxiety
pleading for me to get back order
venus and neptune wove themselves
into my broken thoughts
the sun showed no mercy
the world deprived me of the stars

yet no matter if i loved you
the moon kept wandering off
to fix broken hearts with its
magical moon dust, there's no stopping it
no revival of the order that once was
the planets squirm in anger
as the moon creates a spike in their manner

for decades, we hope
we hope to someday gleam in the skies
to feel the stars shining against our skin
to live amongst the planets we revise

we hope to exist in eternal beauty
the constellations whirling around our spine
yet the moon gives it all away
shuts the moments into the black hole
as it reeks desperation, for its own hope

hope to fix love, because
those moments when you
lay on his shoulder and
together you admire the moon,
time leaves you alone, suddenly lost track
well in those moments, the moon admires back.

Why Saturn hates Mars

She resembles a ray of sunlight,
for she is comforting and warm.
She is desired by many,
but she belongs to only one.
She has illuminating spirits,
and she shelters the ones in need.
She is capable of life,
to inhabit humans or a seed.

He has cruel intentions,
for he is irritable and miserable.
He is vile in manner,
his heart wholly fictional.
He is cold like ice,
freezing anyone who dares to approach.
He is full of envy,
his breath capable of turning wind to stone.

A séance in the sky, the sun against the moon
Mercury is her May, and Jupiter is his June.

black fills my skies

the metal pipes on the road clatter under my feet
the puddles of mud drown the growing heat
the leaves lace my path as they fall from above
the wind fits my hand like a perfectly suited glove
the sky shows no mercy, surrounding us with clouds
the falling broken branches excrete distressing sounds

i left my water kettle plugged in when i left today
i leave my ac on throughout the month of may
i forgot to turn my car off when
i ran into the gas station for snacks
the dirty grovel stains my feet as
i lay against these isolated train tracks
and reflect, or sympathise, or pity, or plead, or regret

for i have pitied too late, pleaded too little and regretted too soon
the sun hides in its shadows and the sky now hosts the moon
the next morning, the unsettling starts to begin
the grass tries to drain itself, the river loudly cries
my thoughts surround me as now, black fills my skies

a domino effect in the sky

it starts with the tiniest drop of water
barely visible, it camouflages with the air
it progresses to a few drops, now leaving scars
the ground is stained with dots of growth
this tiny drop has now grown into a drizzle
a domino effect in the sky, clouds admire
the flora is satisfied, the deserts feel euphoria
but this drizzle lasts no longer
than the time it takes for a drop to reach the grass
for now, these drops are now blades,
falling from grey clouds
they race to reach the land,
each one faster than the other,
this tiny drop has become a rainfall
it's the valleys who now sing along
with each note these droplets hit
every pitter patter fallen short
because of the now loud thuds
for they are not even loud thuds anymore
in a matter of two seconds
it's now a heavy mountain of tears
in a matter of seconds, this rainfall
grows into a sharp peak
a peak of lost crime, losing all direction
and so, it flies over here,
and flies to the other side
rain is now outnumbering the land
taking over from each corner
the blades of water striking down
now carry the grey clouds along
and thus, the clouds are replacing our winds
the birth of a storm

the burden of the rain

i have lit every tree in this land on fire
i have entangled my guilt in these electrical wires
i have pitted and wilted and cried and screamed
i have pleaded in every way for a chance to redeem
as after diminishing the soil down to each grain
i now have to face the burden of the rain

the rainfall starts soft, every drizzle falling gracefully
the stillness of this atmosphere fills my heart with vacancy
for the timidness of the rain is painful to my spine
the politeness of its actions drives me to intertwine
i do not deserve this pleasantness for i am a monster inside
i beg the clouds to rush, to elevate the speed of time

the rainfall grows heavier, but only enough for a pitter patter
for now, the winds emerge, my plants sway and dishes clatter
the rain has turned its back on me, it is looking away in shame
i let the storm engulf me as i soak up this grass in my blame
but the story is still on its second page, for the rage is yet to come
and until it does, i must sit here and wait for the expiration of my freedom

the seasons are confused

the leaves are now dry, all ready to fall to the ground
the animals going in to hibernate, no ruckus or sound
the grass seems less green, there's no one to admire anymore
the wind is getting deeper, the clouds are now coming low
it's the uncomfortable feeling in-between warm and cold
there are no snowflakes to dance nor the sun to spread its gold
the trees and skies are in confusion, this feeling misunderstood
the smell of dainty flowers is replaced by the smell of hard wood

it's the state between i'm happy and i'm low
when she doesn't want to stay but she doesn't want to go
it's not a moment of sorrow, but more like a boring middle
the leaves finally fall, the fruits nervously fiddle
and so, the trees and fruits; all beauty thinks to itself
is it time to die yet? being pushed at the back of a shelf

there are no christmas lights, no spring flora or summer breeze
the clouds cough in pain, the winds let out a loud wheeze
the people stay in, it's too dull of a time to go out
the children hover for summer shine, they grieve and they pout
there is beauty in the change, the old sunny days forgotten
the state of confusion now has a name, the fire finally out, in autumn

black fills my skies vol. 2 / *"my haunting black shadow"*

my haunting black shadow always follows me around
with every step i take, every word i say, every sound
my haunting black shadow can be seen through the waters
the polluted drains making this lake black and the climate hotter
my haunting black shadow reflects the bruises on the trees
for they have been burnt and abused, broken down to their knees
my haunting black shadow blends in with these cement streets
litter coating the pathway, the plants cry and the grass weeps
my haunting black shadow always follows me around
whether i see it in the waters, the trees, or our very own ground
for man has conquered the land, and what's left
is nothing more than a black shadow

but i accepted all of this, my shadow became a part our land
i stood with patience, bit my tongue as slowly the forest dies
no one saw this as an issue, nothing stopped nothing banned
until the day black started to fill up our skies

the ghosts of summer

summer's ghost casts a shadow on this land
and so the flowers wilt into this graveyard of sand
summer's ghost despises winter's scent
the winds turn into vapour and snow turns into cement

summer's ghost is bitter about the grey clouds
for it leaves the clouds distorted, bouts of dark matter surrounds
summer's ghost is out to get the orange trees
crumbling the remains of the green grass, crippling the yellow leaves

and when the month of may comes around, this town recovers
for we are no longer haunted by the vengeful ghosts of summer

the sun is falling asleep

a drop of honey-dew yellow appears between the clouds
the spotlight grows stronger and winds overcrowd
the silence of the nights sets in, the skies now retire
for now, this pallet of blue is ignited with an orange fire

and so, this warm-pale yellow starts to coat the skies
the droplets of sunlight and flowers turn into allies
humidity replaces the strong relentless winds
and a golden glow reflects onto everyone’s skin

these old-school moments still have their charm
as we sit by the perfectly placed roses near the pond
for we experience this moment in each other’s arms
as we watch the calm and benevolent blue skies turn blonde

i broke my own heart by mistake

yesterday the sun didn't shine inside my room
my pillows and my sheets cursed all my sins
for my dead flowers were settled and ready to bloom
my antibodies starting to attack me from within

the grass grazed my naked feet as i roamed in circles on the sand
the stone in the mud mixing with my blood as i drain into the land

the glass of water by the sink was full of all my envy
my chest muscles exhale yet my body gets more heavy
the veins wrapping my heart, contain its loud cries
our fingers twisted together, slowly pull to untie

my bones rush to hurt me, as they poke out of my sides
the welcome mat on my doorstep cannot look me in the eyes
as everyone and everything knows that i am to blame
i broke my own heart, my mirrors filling with vain

as my evil comes out, my body is the one who suffers
silence fills the atmosphere as my thoughts stop to buffer
they scream and they cry, no one understands this complication
the grimy books on my shelf are at a loss for comprehension

the leaves pull out their pigment
my heart slows down its rhyme
my blood restores in my ligament
the clock rewinds the time

yesterday the sun didn't shine inside my room
my windows deprived me, as darkness started to consume
to consume the entirety of my body, every speck and every flake
i'm sorry, i plead. i broke my own heart by mistake.

alcohol within your lips

you stand, bottle in hand, the substance within your lips
you say you can live without it, no big deal, it's just a drink,
something you sip on to help you get by on hard days
but when those hard days turn into months and the sip is now two glasses
when the two glasses become four and your family no longer glances
no glancing and staring, they know it's just the usual
the usual, the regular, the everyday routine
you are no longer yourself, but this you cannot see
because your eyes are half closed and your words are slurred
you're walking in crooked lines and your vision is blurred
you add another ice cube, just enough to numb your hand
this is now the life you lead, it is not as you planned
the day that drink became more than just something you sip on
the day you lost your friends, your family, yourself
the day you admit it—you need it, some help
the day it all changed, when the drink was no longer for pleasure
it was to take away all the pain, the feeling, the pressure
it takes away the edge, just enough, stopping Icarus's fall—
it doesn't end the suffering, just delays it, it stalls
open your eyes, realise you are on the tip
you stand, bottle in hand, alcohol within your lips.

misery loves company *(and i love you)*

misery loves company, sorrow entices joy
hatred drowns in love, gratification strives to annoy
timidness tries to be loud, music reeks silence
uncertainty is comforting, healing requires violence
in order to break into two one must first offer their whole
her body left bruised with burns and scarred by the cold

unhappiness blesses those in lust
from us to you and me, from smoke to dust
but we still have each other, luckily
for they say, misery loves company

terminal lucidity

his heartbeat monitor started to alarm
the tumultuous sound, a presage of the end
and so, i leaned in and laid in his arms
our love adjoins and our hatred makes amends

for once he is awake, he will be asleep again
i grasp at the withering strings of hope
and after his last heartbeat, my wounds will be deep again
as his blood will soon dry and nature will take its course

this concept is so complex,
yet we feel nothing but simplicity
for we spend our last moments together
in this state of terminal lucidity

death became her

she was soft-spoken before this fire ignited her rage
she was sympathetic before she was forced into this cage
she was kindhearted before evil distorted her manner
she was my safe space before she fell in love with the dagger

for there were times we'd fear our demise
she was scared of spiders, i was scared of fireflies
yet her fear of dying became more and more uncertain
as now in her eyes, i am nothing but an intolerable burden

and now i stay, remembering the times of what we once were
for the day came when she didn't die, but rather *death became her.*

why women kill

she killed everyone he did
but backwards and in high heels
she keyed his car with a death threat
and deflated his wheels
there's a lipstick stain of her
under his excuse for being late
for now, he has let this *other woman*
trap him from his fate

but women are nurturing and elegant
we do not indulge in such petty crimes
so, when she murders you,
i promise she will be delicate
and make sure to kiss you goodbye

and we do it with discretion
his heartbeat now at a still
the day-old question
of why women kill

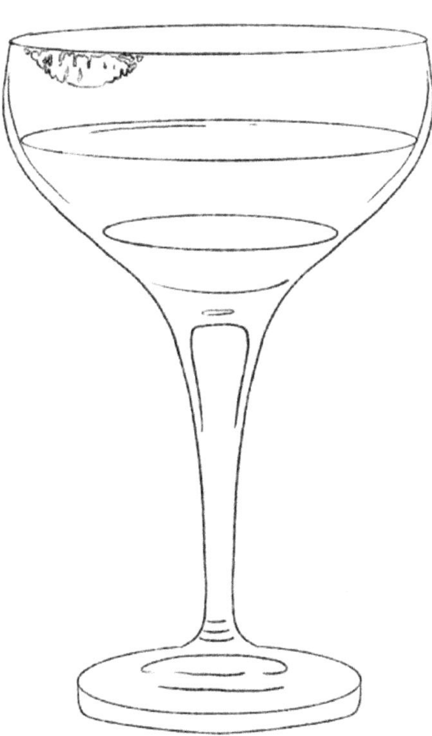

practically lethal in every way

our love was a personification of poetry
our love was full of passion and rage
our love found home under the rowan tree
our love was not restricted by its cage

our love was a game for two
our love adored the attention
our love started with me and ended with you
our love was often a point of contention

our love put me to bed every night
our love shared moments with our pain by the river
our love calmed you down after heated fights
our love gave me warmth when i felt a slight shiver

our love was co-dependent
our love was violent at times
our love was an antique silver pendant
our love was a dirty watch coated in grime

and while i remember the times we spent
all the envy we felt every day
now i understand our love was
practically lethal in every way

cry me a river & i'll dry it out

if you are gasping for air, begging me while you choke
i will light a fire and turn this oxygen into smoke
if you give me your heart, i will make sure it breaks
if you need water, i will steal the contents of the lake
if you need my silence, i will scream and shout
and so, if you cry me a river, i'll dry it out

gaslight

a dying fire, a small orange glow
the flare gasping for breath
the heat dissolving into the coal
and now small sparks remain
hidden under the cigarette ash
but you come with your lighter in hand
and words full of fuel gas

da vinci was a fraud

cameras flash in excitement
crowds gather to admire
artists succumb to the enticement
for da vinci was the coal which lit this fire

a wooden frame bounds it
thirty by twenty-one inches
a mountain of security surrounds it
every country desires its riches

Lisa del Giocondo they call her
the most beautiful woman to ever exist
her expressions strike with a spur
every brush stroke perfectly flattens, flows, twists

and as you watched her,
i watched you
and in that moment i knew
mona lisa's beauty
is nothing compared to you

when you reach the end of this poem, let her memory go

an army of apple trees attack my aching pains
broken bluebells infiltrate the working of my brain
creeping charcoal cables capture my collar bones
delirious depression pills multiply in their dose
every effect on me endures the eagerly growing evil
for my forearms fabricate and fingernails fortify
gallons of fuel gas drowned me when we last said goodbye
helplessly i pleaded, my hands weak and happiness weaker,
i succumb instantly, the ice inside me ignites an imploding fever
justifying these jarring actions with the excuse of your joy
kernels of rage keenly knot into my knees, creating their decoy
learning love doesn't last forever, something i've grown to know
my madness appearing miniature against your meretricious glow
now that you've reached the end of this poem, let her memory go

Five questions I don’t want you to answer

what would you do if sunlight disappeared?
if she no longer gave you warmth
no longer dried our land
forgot about our flowers
didn’t turn wet soil into soft sand

who would you be without the blessing of the rain?
in the anxious anticipation of the storm
the wind exhales and breath becomes stone
for the rain no longer comforts you
rather is the one who isolates you alone

where would you run if the wind kept chasing?
through the forests and into the rivers
from underwater to the highest altitudes
for as long as you can run, the wind can chase
a solemn procession, stripped of your gratitude

when would you realise the world turned grey?
you no longer see colour around
no longer find beauty in our flowers,
appreciate the sphere in the sky,
see a shadow against the ground

why would you bother if autumn went away?
for no hope is left, the leaves are left yellow
winter will never come, but summer doesn’t last
why bother in trying, why even ask?

a night at windy pharaoh

the walls are cemented with grains of gypsum
the hallway is coated in distant reminiscence
the glass chandelier reflects tiny droplets of light
the check-in counter stands towering over me

my eyes wander from corner to corner of this old motel
as the night grew older, the ambience in the lobby steadily fell
i catch a glimpse of the bell-boy, pillars of marble hinder my view
the carpet beneath me dissolves the dust stuck in my shoes

the bright neon sign on the door lured me in
for not many people cross this part of town
but on this cold night in the suburbs asheville
i find myself within this hidden gem which surrounds

— *the windy pharaoh motel*

sharks

forever I have heard
to never look back
that looking back will only stop me
only hinder my growth

forever I have been told
to be like a shark
who always swims forward
who always gets what it wants

but I ask them back
that isn't it true
the reason we catch the shark
is because it *never* looks back

From Slovakia

coquelicot curtains are mounted on the doors
a cry for help withdraws from the cemented walls
implicit carvings envelope every inch of this house
for the gardens grow orchids, strings of apricots sprout

bryndzové pirohy is served on a silver plate
the sugar-cane fields extend for illimitable miles
the towns are rather tiny, the inhabitants rather peculiar
the automobiles are small in number, factories even fewer

yet this land requires no advancement
the city lives peacefully in its natural state
every morning the flea market fills with new fruits
freshly picked apples, home-grown viscid dates

if you do not drown in the mountains, you will forfeit to the ice
you may get sick of it, but you will never succumb to boredom
for there are a labyrinth of caves and a castle at every corner
Medzilaborce worships Warhol, their gin replaces the water

the world revolves around that postcard
you sent me from the last time in Slovakia
the souvenir cut open, extirpated, and charred
and so her land remains in my fondness of my heart

the tea vendors of new delhi

in the hidden corners of the noisiest streets of this bustling city
the ambrosial aroma of ground masala chai grains lingers
the ultimate cure for those evenings that are a bit too windy
the noise vanishes as the metal glasses clatter and tea kettles simmer

cardamom, ginger, cloves, black peppercorns and milk
the perfectly curated mixture for your taste buds
and while shopping for houseware or saris of silk
it will lure you in, within the crooked roads and wet mud

for there will always be enough for you
the doses come in plenty
in these hidden corners of the noisy streets live
the tea vendors of new delhi

red riding hood with a gun

a tale told to young minds that are easily influenced
red riding hood could not save herself, a princess needs a prince
but what would have happened if red riding hood had a gun
not a little helpless girl, she can do more than run

on that day when the wolf tried to attack
she held her breath, took a step back
with no hesitance, her finger was on the trigger
overshadowed by the mighty wolf and his big figure
she takes her aim, tightens her grip
fires the pistol, and so, red riding hood lives
not because of a man, a woodsman who was around
this time the girl saved herself, not a cry nor a sound

red riding hood does not need a saviour
the girl with the basket, walking under the sun
all she really needs is her red coat and gun.

game

ever since we arrive
on this cruel earth,
we have been sworn
into a noble birth

is it worth all this pain
all happiness erodes to vapour
with nothing to gain
but a huge pile of paper

is this a successful life
one filled with tremblings of greed
is it worth to have a wife
not to love her but like animals to breed

so tamed are our senses
by etiquette created by a fool
that we can't break down societies' defences
that we believe in being ruled

to heaven no money will go through
no title or debt or mistakes to undo
but your soul with its pride and its name
and the role you played in this game

the times in which my perfect gpa cannot help

there is no formula for love
i cannot turn my emotions into
algebraic expressions and solve

my feelings are not backed up
by definitions in physics
i can't express my emotions
through logic; through science

yes, my body works as taught in
biology but that does not explain
the wars in my brain between my thoughts
for i'm constantly fighting against my own self

i cannot use statistics from a
business perspective because
my cries are outnumbered
in socially awkward situations
i cannot apply chemicals to
get a different reaction

although history teaches us about dictators
how to control a population with totality
i cannot quote hitler's speeches to manipulate
situations in which i find myself lost

when my family is let down,
i cannot use geography to find
a new place to drown myself

yet, when my emotions need to be
expressed, solved, worked out:
i turn to english

— expression through poetry,
for words will never abandon me

king

like every boy, i have grown up
dreaming of being a knight
for the chance to prove
my pride and valour
the chance to prove myself
a worthy saviour

like every girl, i have grown up
begging to be a princess
craving the perfect ending,
the story with a happily ever after

like everyone, i have grown up
wanting to be a king
to have all the power in the land,
to control everything

but now that i am all grown up
i see the terrible truth that
you can never be a knight
with no blood on your hands
you can never be a princess
with her dreams fulfilled
and you can never be a king
with a sane mind

scars

could you imagine if the
earth had perfect skin,
ask yourself
where would the fish swim?
where would we climb?
where would the ladybugs live?
where would we pose with our fake smiles?
is it worth it, to give up all
that makes our land beautiful?

we are not flawless
and neither is the land we walk upon
there lies beauty in our scars
for every blemish in our skin
resembles the holes in our stars

Flaming butterflies

It starts with a butterfly
just flying around
it goes unnoticed
no trace; no sound

it calls its companions
and they fly about
it feels different around him
but you still have doubts

And then they set themselves alight
and now it's your turn
every inch of your body knows
that it's time to burn

The flaming butterflies consume
that space in your chest
they take all the reasoning away
and you forget the rest

And they remember you
for your smoking heart
that flaming soul of yours
that made you different; apart

lust, passion, love

she turns around to catch your eye
a woman you've never seen before
before your heart can even deny
you're sprawled across the wooden floors
from above, desire laughs and heat flares
and down below, no one speaks about
what happened underneath the stairs
and you know that without a doubt
you'll remember her for her kiss
rather than who she is
then, my dear, you've fallen in lust

she turns around to catch your eye
and a flame ignites within you
your heart flies, coating red into the sky
your mind now burning a hole through
you instantly understand how important she is
and you know another realised that too
but your heart would be as sad as his
if you weren't there for their I do's
for she is but a friend, the one who drives you
the yellow ember which taints your navy hue
then, my dear, you've fallen in passion

she turns around to catch your eye
your heart goes out of control
and before you can even comply
you've fallen down the rabbit hole
and you start together, first as friends
then slowly it becomes a little more
and finally, then the hand extends
and the dress is out of the store
you know you both belong in each other's arms
away from the lures of false charms
then, my dear, you've fallen in love

when your flowers have wilted and the sun has said its goodbyes

look for me when the pages in this book start to corrode
when the winds capture our trees and lakes spill into our roads
look for me when the first petal of the carnation i gave you turns brown
when the atmosphere is burdened with pity, the koi fish in our pool drown
look for me on a sunny wednesday afternoon at the crowded market
when i lay freshly picked cherries and the new delivery of siena harvest
look for me by the river bed when the clouds abandon our skies
when your flowers have wilted and the sun has said its goodbyes

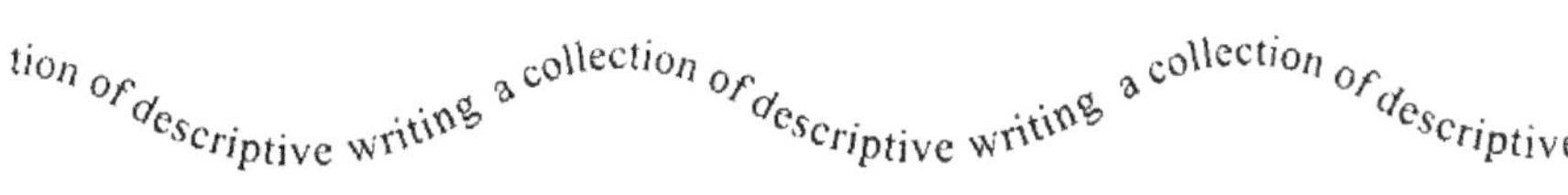

sserie amandine / a sunday morning in an all american diner / eclipse

Pâtisserie Amandine.

The auburn wooden flooring creaks with each step which lands on it. The vibrant pink fabric used for the curtains were perfectly matched with the long sofa which frames the right side of this room. Each layer of fabric perfectly coils at the ends of the drapes, and a bow ties it to each side as it makes way for the sun. The windows are panelled by white polished wood, the window stills are rigid from not being opened in years.

Pâtisserie Amandine was located on the second floor of an old French building, the first was occupied by a small bookstore, ran by Missure Fleur; he was old, he was spiteful, he was unwelcoming, and he was callous. He would snarl at almost every customer approaching the staircase to the cafe above. Still, Pâtisserie Amandine was sold out almost every single day. Busy work lunches, early morning coffee runs, late night soirées, you name it.

Fresh tablecloths were laid every morning, the sides were embroidered by pastel yellow and blue strings as they flowed into shapes of striking flowers and elaborate animals. The tablecloth was dressed with the most elegant silverware, the forks and spoons had carvings of seashells by the handle. Each plate, knife, fork, spoon, and napkin had to be placed in the most precise manner, as perfection calls for attention to miniature details. Each table also featured a basket of bread, the scent making the customer's lips drool from the moment they take a seat. The decor for Pâtisserie Amandine was classic in all its sense, the French revolution inspired the walls and the satin covering the chairs were rich in style, as if Marie Antoinette herself picked them out. Let them eat cake, she says.

Pastries of all kinds were displayed by the glass bar. Strawberry shortcakes, lemon sorbets, chocolate mousses, vanilla parfaits, and the most delicious croissants. However, if Pâtisserie Amandine had a speciality, it would be the homemade ice cream. Milk from the hills of Sweden, tangerines picked from Moscazzano and sugar from the foothills of Punjab; whirled together, combined into a sweet-tasting sorbet served at the counter in a petite paper cup. Visitors restlessly anticipated their chance to feel the sensation of the cold, crushed ice on their palates.

Pâtisserie Amandine is a home to the locals of this small city in France, tourists from ends of the world and Missure Fleur, for he enjoyed his evening cup of coffee by the window of this café; occasionally even smiling after the first sip.

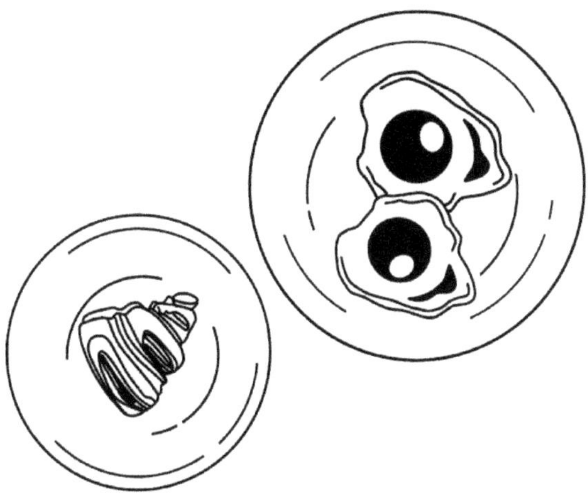

A Sunday morning in an all American diner.

A faint aroma of the strong earthy smell of the Columbian coffee beans brewing in the kitchen fills up the tight air space of this five hundred square foot diner. Every perfectly polished tile on the floor matches the velvet curtains, screening the heat from melting the metal knobs on the doors. The velvet curtains are hung up, as by itself it causes too much darkness. Instead, it is angled at the perfect arch to block the rampaging rays of light but still hold up the perfect golden hue during Sunday mornings here. The hazel leather seats cushion the many who spend their afternoons working here. Every crinkle in the skin of the leather, is one of experience of the past sixty-two years. The metal knobs match the metal stands of the tables. Four perfect cylinders hold up the panel of light ombre wood. The tables neatly scrubbed every morning, for the day brings many coasters and crumbs. The two steps to walk into this peculiar diner have a story to them as well, for the dented edges have seen numerous wheelchairs back in the day. Opened in 1958, if the archaic decor doesn't give it away, perhaps the neon sign on the gate will. Of course, any American diner is incomplete without its neon sign. The fluorescent red tubes, glaring at every pedestrian, luring them into coming inside. The windows are tinted with a vibrant blue, making every day look pleasant even if in reality the clouds are heaving in the skies. The workers giving a performance as hosting is not only an income to them, but a passion as well. All smiles from the moment the menu is handed to you till the wave you receive as you walk out the door. The golden polished bell on the marble counter dings. "Two sunny side ups with a side of sausages ready for table 12!" the chef exclaims with excitement as every dish finished provides the same satisfaction as completing a work of art. This diner sees a lot of exciting days, and a few gloomy ones. But no matter the circumstance, you will see that 'closed' sign plastered against the glass entrance door flip, turning to 'open' the next morning at seven am.

Eclipse

My thoughts are scrambling to be heard through this ocean filled with people drowning away the voices in my head. The crowd, leaking out in bits to the sidewalk as thousands wait in anticipation in their perfectly picked spots for the sun to elope with the moon. Through nudging elbows and threats of terror, many climb treetops and curved rocks to get the most precise angle. Human nature is strange, many clueless of what this astronomical moment even signifies. Yet every beating heart in this garden longs for the feeling of saying "I saw it, it was right in front of me." The opportunity to boast overshadows the burden of obliviousness that fills up this space in every corner. The people who have studied this topic, rambled their minds through pages and pages of encrypted information on the matter of every star have been pushed to the back while the saleswomen and firefighters string together in the first row. Followed by the musicians, the painters, every type of person you could imagine neglects their place in this silent town to cluster up against the roots of the trees in this garden. As the mummers slow down, a slight movement is felt by every eye blinking here. My eyelashes in a race with each other, fluttering up and down as I try to pretend like I see a difference at all. Cameras are pointed, the restless kids are being hushed.

Everybody's skin was laced with golden imprints of the raging sun. The anger storms out, as flames of fire burn the waxy layer on every growing leaf. In an instance, the golden rays are slowly being replaced by a deep shadow, soaking in every drop of optimism in this town. The sun shines proud, gifting every grain of sand in the street with its lustful presence. Yet at this moment we stand, as the moon steals away its pride. A séance in the sky, the clouds darken in colour as this shadow spins around your spine, trying to release all of your past trauma. This crowd at a loss for words, the loud ambience is now lacking the sound of breaths. Not a word is left to be said, darkness is furiously racing in from every corner, a stampede of melancholy breaks out in this space. Your eyes wish to look away but in this moment as the moon falls in love with the sun, the romance of their love is a terror to the town. This intimacy for two, is darkness for thousands. People's expressions speak volumes, their mouths wide enough to hold all of the world's contents. Our eyes open as if the pupils have been replaced by stone. Out of the corner of my cornea, a ray of golden light seeps through the back of this growing shadow. The light creeks through, creating a crescent now. For the moon floats away and the sun replicates its manner. In seconds, the light regains its place and fills up the air as the holes fill up in soil and roads shed their pebbles. Every mouth in this space coils its way into a grin. Noises of cheer and envy arise as the sun is now the star on the stage of the sky.

a note from me to you:

thank you for making it till the end.

here lies three years of poetry and writing

from my scrambled late night thoughts and

endless coffee shop writing sessions

i leave you with my first book —

when flowers wilt

<3

www.ingramcontent.com/pod-product-compliance
Ingram Content Group UK Ltd.
Pitfield, Milton Keynes, MK11 3LW, UK
UKHW021935190726
13853UKWH00004B/1449

9 789354 721595